The Far Side GALLERY 4

by Gary Larson

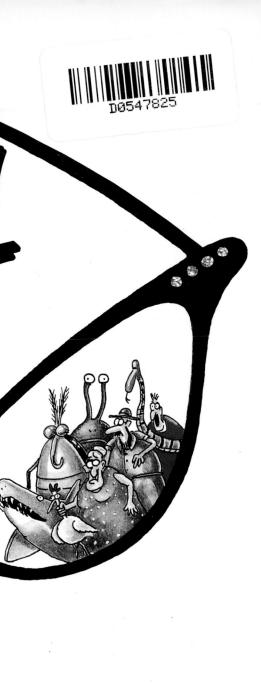

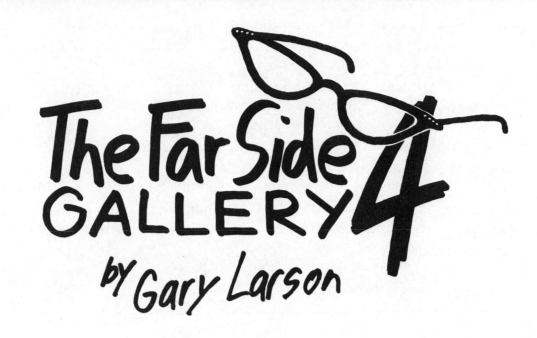

The Far Side Gallery 4

by Gary Larson

WARNER BOOKS

A Warner Book

First published in Great Britain in 1993 by Warner Books
Reprinted in 1993 (twice), 1994 (three times), 1995 (twice), 1996.

The Far Side is a cartoon feature created by Gary Larson and
distributed internationally by Universal Press Syndicate. This book was first published in the United
States by Andrews and McMeel.

A CIP catalogue record for this book
is available from the British Library.

ISBN 0 7515 0813 6

Printed and bound in Great Britain by St Ives (Andover) Ltd .
Printed on Reece Hi-white (acid free).

Warner Books
A Division of
Little, Brown and Company (UK)
Brettenham House
Lancaster Place
London WC2E 7EN

The author would like to thank Donna Pickert-Korris, for her art direction and painting expertise;
and Rollie Swanson and Katrina Heckerson for their painting assistance.

When I was a boy, our house was filled with monsters. They lived in the closets, under the beds, in the attic, in the basement, and—when it was dark—just about everywhere.

This book is dedicated to my father, who kept me safe from all of them.

Foreword

Gary Larson is to cartooning what JoJo the Dogfaced Boy is to circus freaks. He's the best of a weird breed. I suppose most people have this image of a cartoonist as a quiet person sitting in a cozy den, puffing on a pipe, and carefully drawing on a sketch pad. Sort of like Norman Rockwell. My image of Gary is more like Norman Bates. I imagine Gary in a dark and mysterious laboratory with chemicals brewing and static electricity crackling. He stands over his sketch pad, cackling like a mad scientist. He raises his arms to the sky. Lightning strikes. And he maniacally shouts, "Give my creation LIFE!!!"

Whenever I read The Far Side I feel like I'm watching a *National Geographic* special on Prozac—talking sharks, cigar-smoking termites, lustful flies, squirrels in cop uniforms, cows with attitudes. I picture Gary wandering through zoos and aquariums, talking to all the animals and insects like a demented Dr. Doolittle. He approaches a boll weevil, hands it a contract, and says, "I'd like to sketch you for my next cartoon. Who's your agent?"

But I really love the Larson flair for drawing humans. Future civilizations may dig up his cartoons in archaeological expeditions. Their scientists will examine them and they'll think twentieth century man was a lumpy troglodyte with bad eyesight, buck teeth, and cowlicks. Then again, maybe that's how we *will* evolve. If that's the case—if mankind evolves into a bizarre Gary Larson creation—it's gonna be a strange and funny future.

And, for me, it will be a future with more job security knowing that Gary chose to use a pen rather than a microphone.

Enjoy. I always do.

ROBIN WILLIAMS

"Well, this is just going from bad to worse."

Bullknitters

The deadly couch cobra—coiled and alert in its natural habitat

After flicking on the light, Professor Zurkowitz is caught off guard by the overnight success of his efforts to crossbreed flying fish and piranhas.

Hours later, when they finally came to, Hal and Ruby groggily returned to their yard work—unknowingly wearing the radio collars and ear tags of alien biologists.

Monster jobs

Early piñatas

"Fellow octopi, or octopuses ... octopi? ... Dang, it's hard to start a speech with this crowd."

"Wait a minute! ... McCallister, you fool! *This* isn't what I said to bring!"

The parenting advantages of dentists

How the human egg is often deceived.

"Henry! Our party's total chaos! No one knows when to eat, where to stand, what to. ... Oh, thank God! Here comes a border collie!"

"So then I says to Borg, 'You know, as long as we're under siege, one of us oughta moon these Saxon dogs.'"

Saturday mornings in cockroach households

Headhunter hutwarming

"Well, there he is, Bobby—Big Red. Sure he's tough, but if you can ride him, he's yours."

At the hospital for mothers whose children stepped on sidewalk cracks

Charlie Parker's private hell

In the Chicken Museum

God makes the snake

"Well, scratch No. 24. He did pretty good, though—
right up to the jet engine test."

Although skilled with their pillow arsenal, the Wimpodites were favorite targets of Viking attacks

The spitting cobras at home

Scenes from the entomology underworld

"No doubt about it, boys. See these markings on the bottom? This is an *Apache* pie pan!"

Early settlers of Beverly Hills

Morning in the crypt

"Why'd you do it, Biff? I mean, I always knew car chasing was in your blood—but the president's limo?"

"You know, I used to like this hobby. ... But shoot! Seems like *everybody*'s got a rock collection."

"And, as amoebas, you'll have no problems recruiting other sales reps ... just keep dividing and selling, dividing and selling."

"Take a good, long look at this. ... We don't know what it is, but it's the only part of the buffalo we don't use."

And so it went, night after night, year after year. In fact, the Hansens had been in a living hell ever since that fateful day the neighbor's "For Sale" sign had come down and a family of howler monkeys had moved in.

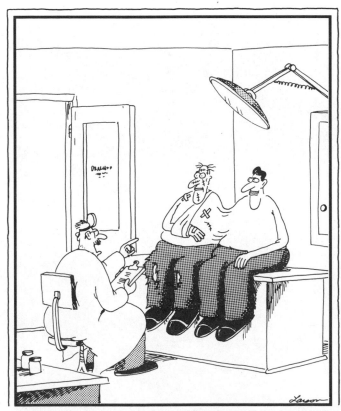

"Wait, wait, wait ... I'm confused. Bob, *you're* the one who's claiming your Siamese twin, Frank, changes into a werewolf every full moon?"

Mountain families

"No, no, no! What are you doing? ... Fifth leg! Fifth leg!"

"Pretty cool, Dewey. ... Hey! Shake the jar and see if they'll fight!"

"You're so morbid, Jonathan—the paper comes, and that's the first section you always head for."

Competition in nature

"Oh my God! It's Leonard! ... He's stuffed himself."

Pinocchio in his later years

Young Victor Frankenstein stays after school.

"So ... they tell me you're pretty handy with a gun."

Lemmings on vacation

"The carnage out here is terrible, Sandy ... feathers everywhere you—Oh, here we go! The Animal Control Officer is leading the so-called Chicken Coop Three away at this very moment."

His rifle poised, Gus burst through the door, stopped, and listened. Nothing but the gentle sound of running water and the rustling of magazines could be heard. The trail, apparently, had been false.

When dogs go to work

Daddy longleg jerks

Another photograph from the Hubble telescope

Front porch forecasters

"I can't believe it! This is impossible! Nothing here but—
wait! Wait! I see something! ... Yes! There they are—
granola bars!"

Embedded in Styrofoam "shoes," Carl is sent to
"sleep with the humans."

"Well, here we go, another exciting evening at the 'Murdocks', all of us sitting around going, 'Hello, my name is so-and-so. ... What's your name? ... I wanna cracker. Hello, my name is so-and-so.'"

"Roy, you get up on the hotel roof there—and for godsakes, if you *are* plugged, don't just slump over and die. Put some drama into it and throw yourself screaming from the edge."

"Yo! Everyone down there! This is the jackal! I'm tired of slinking around in the shadows! ... I'm coming down to the kill! Is that gonna be cool with everyone! ... I don't want trouble!"

An instant later, both Professor Waxman and his time machine are obliterated, leaving the cold-blooded/warm-blooded dinosaur debate still unresolved.

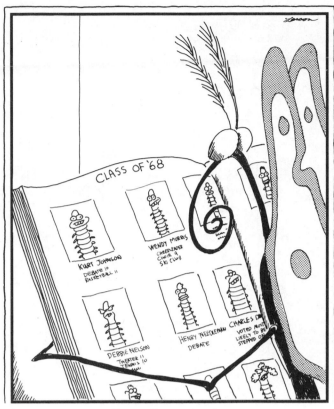

Butterfly yearbooks

Primitive UFOs

Becoming a rogue in his later years, Dumbo terrorized the world's flyways.

At the international meeting of the
Didn't Like *Dances With Wolves* Society

"Why, thank you. ... Thank you very much!"

"I say we do it ... and trichinosis be damned!"

Suddenly, second-chair granite rock's jealousy of first-chair granite rock becomes uncontainable.

Practicing his skills wherever possible, Zorro's younger and less astute brother, Gomez, had a similar career cut short.

Life among the clover

Why people named Buddy hate to drive

Tragedy struck when Conroy, his mind preoccupied with work, stepped into the elevator—directly between a female grizzly and her cub.

"Tell it again, Gramps! The one about being caught in the shark frenzy off the Great Barrier Reef!"

Although nervous, the Dickersons were well-received by this tribe of unique headhunters. It was Pooki, regrettably, that was to bear the brunt of their aggression.

Cowmen Miranda

Infamous moments in jazz

Dog restaurants

The crew of the Starship Enterprise encounters the floating head of Zsa Zsa Gabor.

"Well, here's your problem, Marge—if you and Bob really want kids, next time try sittin' on these little guys."

"OK, Zukutu—that does it! Remember, those who live in grass houses shouldn't throw spears."

Wildlife day shifts

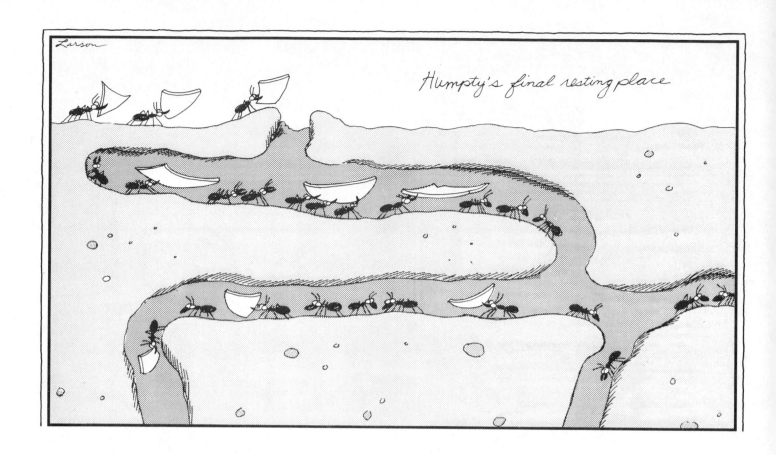

Humpty's final resting place

"Zelda! Cool it! ... The Rothenbergs hear the can opener!"

"Aaaaaa! There goes another batch of eggs, Frank! ... No wonder this nest was such a deal."

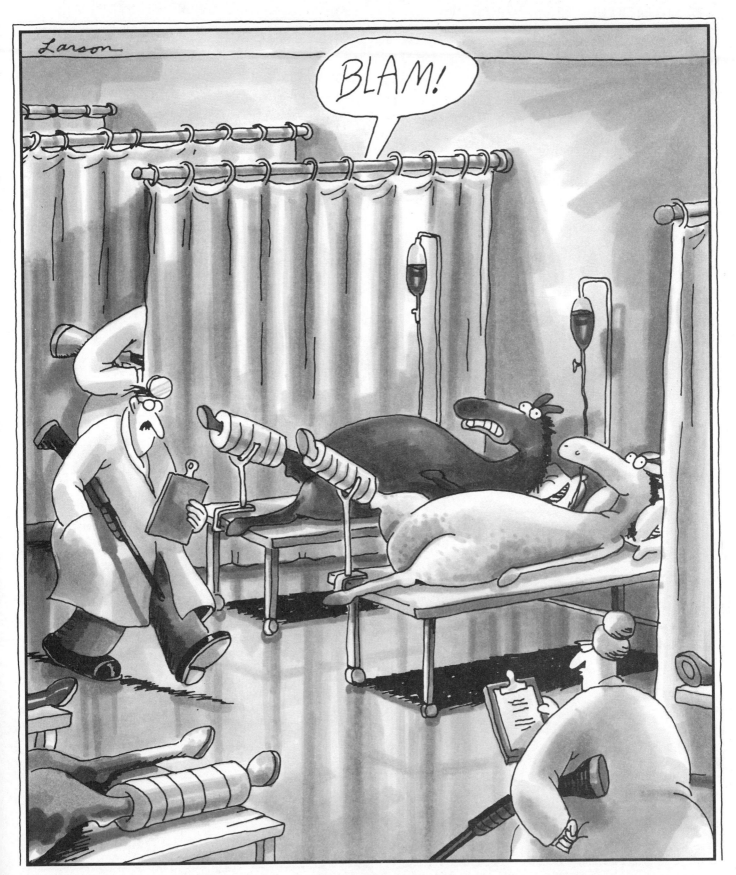

Horse hospitals

Inconvenience stores

"Careful, Lyle! ... There's some cattle dancing!"

Innovative concepts in exposing city kids to nature

Hooting excitedly, primitive scientists Thak and Gork try out their new "Time Log."

The fake McCoys

Accountant street gangs

For a very brief period, medieval scientists were known to have dabbled in the merits of cardboard armor.

In sudden disgust, the three lionesses realized they had killed a tofudebeest—one of the Serengeti's obnoxious health antelopes.

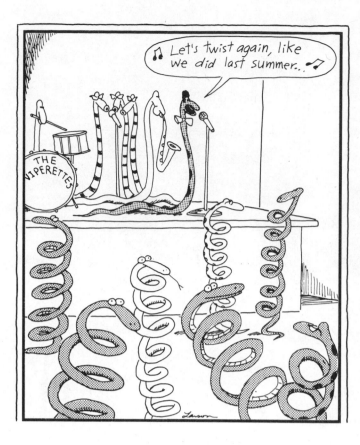

Although it lasted only 2 million years, the Awkward Age was considered a hazardous time for most species.

"I'm afraid it's bad news, Mr. Griswold. ... The lab results indicate your body cavity is stuffed with a tasty, bread-like substance."

At the Old Cartoonists' Home

Life in the primordial soup

The growing field of animal liposuction

Stephen King's childhood ant farm

Tethercat

Fool school

"Whoa! Whoa! Whoa! ... You're in my favorite chair again, Carl."

"You ever do this? ... Just sit in a place like this and antwatch?"

Hibernating Eskimos

The Secret Elephant Aerial Grounds

"Well, we could go back to my place, but you have to understand—I'm *serious* when I say it's just a hole in the wall."

"Don't worry ... your little boy's somewhere in our service department—but let's move on and check out the TD500."

George Washington: general, president, visionary, break dancer.

Ralph Harrison, king of salespersons

"The wench, you idiot! Bring me the *wench*!"

Slug vacation disasters

Deer Halloweens

The rooster stared back at me, his power and confidence almost overwhelming. Down below, a female paused warily at the coop's entrance. I kept the camera running. They were beautiful, these "Chickens in the Mist."

Primitive fraternities

Cockroach nightmares

Professor Lundquist, in a seminar on compulsive thinkers, illustrates his brain-stapling technique.

As a child, little Henry Jekyll would often change himself into a big, red-haired delinquent that parents in the neighborhood simply dubbed "that Hyde kid."

"Now, this is our dead beetle room, and some of these babies are 50 times an ant's body weight. ... 'Course, we'll want to start you out on dried ladybugs."

"Well, here we go again. ... Did anyone here *not* eat his or her homework on the way to school?"

"Ooooooweeeeee! This thing's been here a loooooooong time. Well, thank God for ketchup."

"Oh, my! Cindy! This looks exquisite! ... And look, Frank—isn't that a cheeseball stuffed in its mouth?"

"Oh, I don't know. Billy's been having trouble in school, and Sally's always having some sort of crisis. I tell you, Edith, it's not easy raising the dead."

"Bobby, jiggle Grandpa's rat so it looks alive, please."

You never see it coming.

"Hey, everyone! Simmons here just uttered a discouraging word!"

Suddenly, to Rodney's horror, the police arrived with nerd-sniffing dogs.

Thag Anderson becomes the first fatality as a result of falling asleep at the wheel.

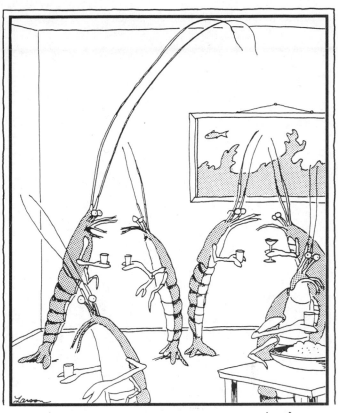

"Listen, you want to come over to my place? I get great FM."

Randy Schueler and his wingless butterfly collection

Anatidaephobia: The fear that somewhere, somehow, a duck is watching you.

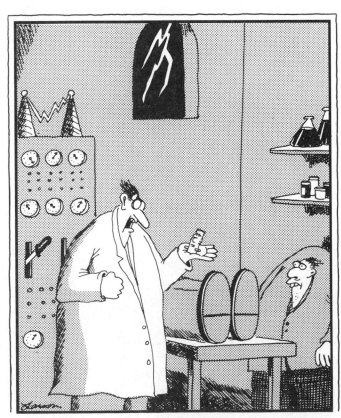

"For crying out loud, Igor! First there's that screw-up with the wrong brain business, and *now* you've let his head go through the wash in your pants' pocket!"

"Mr. Cummings? This is Frank Dunham in Production. ... We've got some problems. Machine No. 5 has jammed, several of the larger spools have gone off track, the generator's blown, and, well, everything seems to be you-know-what."

Although history has long forgotten them, Lambini & Sons are generally credited with the Sistine Chapel floor.

"Well, we've done everything we can; now we can only wait and see if she pulls through. ... If she doesn't, however, I got dibs on these ribs right here."

What really happened to Tinkerbell

Hell's Cafeteria

Far Side Lite: Not funny, but better for you.

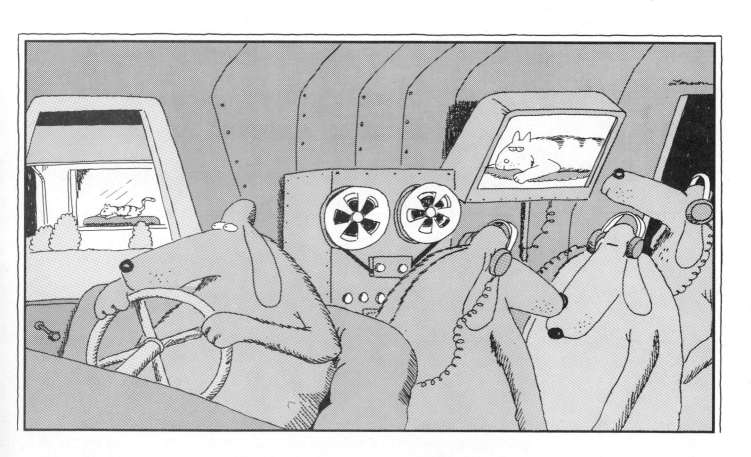

When the monster came, Lola, like the peppered moth and the arctic hare, remained motionless and undetected. Harold, of course, was immediately devoured.

More Facts of Nature: As part of nature's way to help spread the species throughout their ecological niche, bison often utilize a behavior naturalists have described as "ballooning."

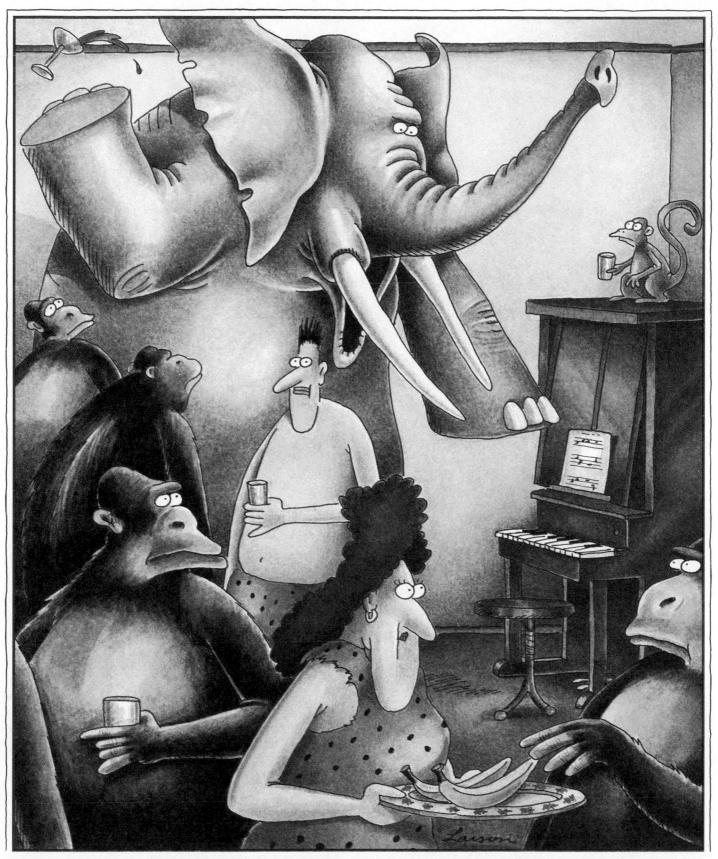

The party had been going splendidly—and then Tantor saw the ivory keyboard.

And down they went: Bob and Francine—two more victims of the La Brea Carpets.

"Well, thank God we all made it out in time. ... 'Course, now we're equally screwed."

The hazards of teaching young Neanderthals

Masher films

The matador's nightmare

"Dang! Every day, more and more swatters are movin' in."

"Oh, no! I have several others—Oggy here is just a tad aggressive, so he has to stay in a cage."

Roger crams for his microbiology midterm.

The dam bursts.

"You know, Vern ... the thought of what this place is
gonna look like in about a week
just gives me the creeps."

"Again? Why is it that the revolution always gets this far
and then everyone just chickens out?"

Early kazoo bands

Aardogs

"OK, ma'am—it's dead. In the future, however, it's always a good idea to check your shoe each time you and the kids return home."

Crossing paths on their respective journeys of destiny, Johnny Appleseed and Irving Ragweed nod "hello."

Thor's hammer, screwdriver, and crescent wrench

Famous patrons of Chez Rotting Carcass

"For crying out loud, Patrick—sit down. ... And enough with the 'give me the potatoes or give me death' nonsense."

"You just take your prey, slip 'em into the flex-o-tube, flip the switch, and the Mr. Coils o'Death takes over."

Baby toys and gifts to avoid this Christmas

"Ticks, fleas ... Ticks, fleas ..."

Until finally being replaced by its more popular and deadly cousin, the Bowie spoon was often used to settle disputes in the Old West.

"Hold it right there, young lady! Before you go out, you take off some of that makeup and wash off that gallon of pheromones!"

Ineffective tools of persuasion

The toaster divers of Pago Pago

"Just ignore him. That's our rebellious young calf Matthew—he's into wearing leather clothes just for the shock value."

"You eat what you've taken, Mitchell. ... I know you're just spreading it around."

The squirrels of Central Park

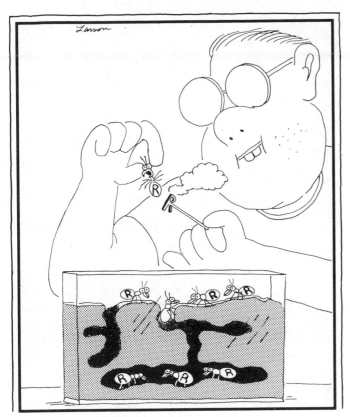

Robby works his ant farm.

Common desert animal tracks

"It's a fax from your dog, Mr. Dansworth.
It looks like your cat."

"Don't worry, Jimmy—they're just actors ... and that's
not real ketchup."

"Drive, Ted! We've stumbled into some cowtown."

Trouble brewing

Animal Waste Management

Buffalo, N.Y., November 2–5: The annual convention of the Big Galoot Society of America.

"Well! No wonder! ... Look who's been loose the whole evening!"

However, there was no question that, on the south side of the river, the land was ruled by the awesome *Tyrannosaurus Mex*.

Early department stores

Houdini's final undoing

Convinced by his buddies that in actual fact they were
only grave "borrowing," a young Igor starts on his
road to crime.

"Oh, man! You must be looking for 'Apartment 3-G,'
'Mary Worth,' or one of those other
'serious' cartoons."

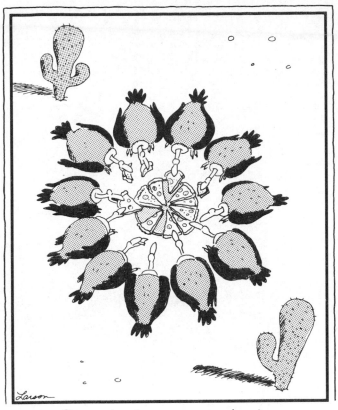

Perspectives in nature we rarely enjoy

"Listen—I bought these here yesterday, and the dang things won't stop squeaking!"

"Dave! Ain't that your horse that kid is messin' with?"

Karl Malden in his basement

The birth of head-hunting

"Uh-oh. Carol's inviting us over for cake, and I'm sure it's just *loaded* with palm oil."

"Well, well—another blond hair. ... Conducting a little more 'research' with that Jane Goodall tramp?"

Medieval pickup battles

The Potatoheads in Brazil

"First of all, Mr. Hawkins, let's put the gun down. ...
I would guess it's an itchy trigger finger, but I want to
take a closer look."

"Make a note of this, Muldoon. ... The wounds seem to
be caused by bird shot ... big bird shot."

A day in the Invisible Man's household

Fleaboys

"Just look at this room—body segments everywhere!"

Leon Redbone's workout video

Fish funerals

"OK, when I say 'draw,' we draw. ... Ready? ... One, two, three—STRAW! ... OK, just checkin' your ears. ... One, two, three—CLAW! ... OK, DRAWbridge! ..."

The party-goers were enjoying themselves immensely— unaware that, across the street in the shadows, a killer waited.

"Sorry, kids—they've got cable, but no pond."

Dinosaur nerds

Tough spiders

"Not bad, but you guys wanna see a *really* small horse?"

Early archaeologists

New York, 1626: Chief of the Manhattan Indians addresses his tribe for the last time.

"Well, this may not be wise on a first date, but I just gotta try your garlic wharf rats."

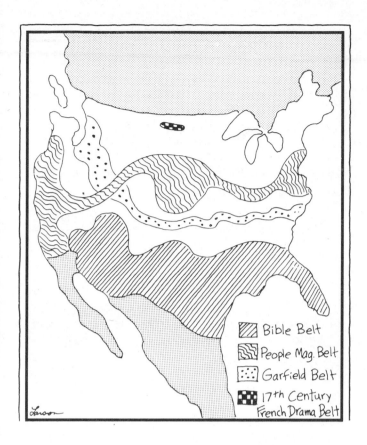

"Criminy! Talk about overstaying your welcome! ... John, open the door and turn the porch light on—see if that gets rid of them."

"The guy creeps me out, Zeena. Sure, he looks like he's just minding his own business—but he always keeps that one eye on my house."

"Yeah, Clem. I hurt. But y'know, it's a *good* kind of hurt."

"Aaaaaaaaaaaaa! Earl! ... We've got a poultrygeist!"

"Now relax. ... Just like last week, I'm going to hold the cape up for the count of 10. ... When you start getting angry, I'll put it down."

And with Johnny's revelation, Mr. Goodman's popularity in the neighborhood suddenly plummeted.

"There he is, Stan! ... On that birch tree, second branch
from the top, and chattering away like crazy! ... I tell
you—first come the squirrels and then come
the squirrel guns."

"Look at this shirt, Remus! You can zip-a-dee-doo-dah all
day long for all I care, but you keep that dang
Mr. Bluebird off your shoulder!"

"C'mon! Keep those stomachs over the handle! Let the fat do the work! ... That's it!"

To his horror, Irving suddenly realized he had failed to check his own boots before putting them on just minutes ago.

"Mayday! Mayday! This is flight 97! I'm in trouble! ... My second engine's on fire, my landing gear's jammed, and my worthless co-pilot's frozen up!"

"Oh, wait, Doreen—don't sit there. ... That chair's just not safe."

Early but unsuccessful practical jokes

Street physicians

Darren's heart quickened: Once inside the home, and once the demonstration was in full swing, a sale was inevitable.

Every hour on the hour, a huge truck, made entirely of pressed ham, lumbers its way across Dog Heaven—and all the car chasers can decide for themselves whether or not to participate.

Full moon and empty head

"Oh, good heavens, no, Gladys—not for me. ... I ate my young just an hour ago."

"Oh, for the love of—there goes Henry! ... Rita, you're closest to him—give that c-clamp about a quarter turn, will ya?"

"Now remember, Cory, show us that you can take good care of these little fellows and maybe *next* year we'll get you that puppy."

"And one more thing about tomorrow's company picnic: Do I have to mention what happened last year when some wise guy sabotaged the games with a case of acid-filled LD-50s?"

"Well, it's a delicate situation, sir. ... Sophisticated firing system, hair-trigger mechanisms, and Bob's wife just left him last night, so you *know* his mind's not into this."

"Joe! You went and ate the pig I was going to serve this evening to the MacIntyres? ... Well, you just disgorge it— it should still be OK."

"And the really great thing about this jungle of ours is that any one of you could grow up to be King of the Apes."

Door Ding Gnomes at Work

"Mom! … Earl's grossing me out with a
mouthful of worms!"

Math phobic's nightmare

"Idiot! ... You're standing on my foot!"

"What? You're just going to throw the tail away? ... Why, in *my* day, we used every goldang *part* of a mammoth!"

Killer bees are generally described as starting out as larvae delinquents.

And for the rest of his life, the young reptile suffered deep emotional scars.

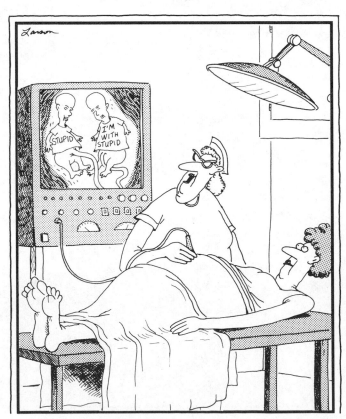

"There you go, Mrs. Eagen—you can clearly see both twins on the monitor."

Inside a nuclear power plant

Scene from *Return of the Nose of Dr. Verlucci*

"OK, Johnson—we've got a deal. We'll let your people and my people work out the details."

"Ben—what d'ya say we turn the power off for a while and let the little guy roam around?"

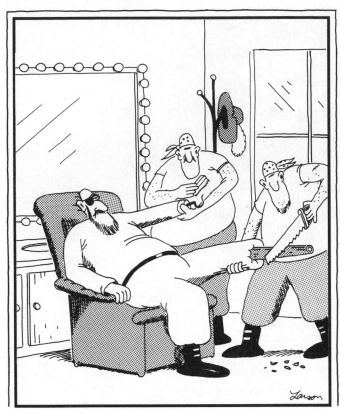

Pirate manicures

The Fullertons demonstrate Sidney's trick knee.

"Listen, before we take this guy, let me ask you this: You ever kill a flea before, Dawkins? It ain't easy."

Each time the click beetle righted itself, Kyle would flip it over again—until something went dreadfully wrong.

"Wait, Morrison! ... It's OK—those are jungle *triangles*!"

"I don't know if this is such a wise thing to do, George."

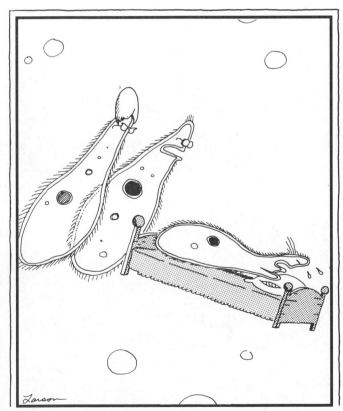

"Now, Betty Sue, we know you're upset ... breaking up with a boyfriend is always hard. But as they say, there are more protozoa in the lower intestine."

March 16, 1942: The night before he leaves the Philippines, General MacArthur works on his farewell address.

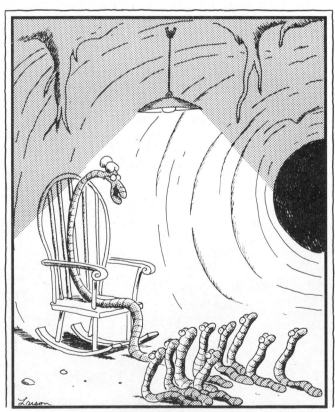

"That story again? ... Well, one stormy night, when the whole family was asleep, your grandfather quietly rose from his bed, took an ax, and made allllllll you little grandkids."

"No *way* am I going to that party tonight! I won't know anyone there, and that means I'll be introduced—*and you know I never learned how to shake!*"

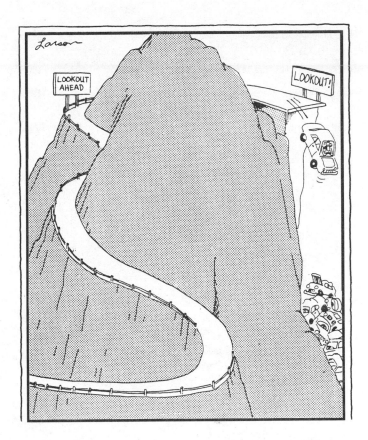

"Yes, yes, I *know* that, Sidney ... *everybody* knows *that*! ... But look: Four wrongs *squared,* minus two wrongs to the fourth power, divided by this formula, *do* make a right."

"Hey! Ernie Wagner! I haven't seen you in, what's it been—20 years! And hey—you've still got that thing growin' outta your head that looks like a Buick!"

"Listen, Mom ... I just wanted you to know I'm OK and the stampede seems about over—although everyone's still a little spooked. Yeah, I know ... I miss the corral."

Trick clubbing exhibitions

The elephant man meets a buffalo gal.

The African Dawn

Whoa! That's plenty.

Carmen Miranda's family reunion

Scene from *Dinner on Elm Street*

Suddenly, Dr. Morrissey's own creation, a hideous creature nine feet tall and bearing the heads of the Brady Bunch, turns against him.

"What the? ... This is lemonade! Where's my culture of amoebic dysentery?"

Cattle drive quartets

"I had them all removed last week and, boy, do I feel great."

"Wow, this place is really packed—or maybe it's just my compound eyes."

It was very late, and Raymond, fighting insomnia, went for a midnight snack. Unfortunately, he never saw the duck blind.

Tapeworms visiting a Stomach Park

Superman in his later years

Ghost newspapers

Suddenly, on a national talk show in front of millions of viewers, Dick Clark ages 200 years in 30 seconds.

Ancient exterminators

"Hey, Bob ... did I scare you or what?"

Saving on transportation costs, some pioneers were known to head west on covered skates.

"I built the forms around him just yesterday afternoon when he fell asleep, and by early evening I was able to mix and pour."

"Did you detect something a little ominous in the way they said, 'See you later'?"

"That does it, Sid. ... You yell 'tarantula' one more time and you're gonna be wearin' this thing."

"Oh God, George! Stop! ... Stop the car! I've got another migration headache!"

It was foolish for Russell to approach the hornets' nest in the first place, but his timing was particularly bad.

"Good heavens, John! Call someone! ... The entire basement looks dry!"

"Well, that's an interesting bit of trivia—I guess I *do* only dream in black and white."

Warren Hagstrom: Professional Western movie background street crosser

"Man, Larry, I don't know if we're up to this. I mean, this guy's got kneecaps from hell."

Saloon scenes on other planets

Studying the African bagel beetle

"You and Fred have such a lovely web, Edna—and I *love* what you've done with those fly wings."

Already concerned, Ernie watched in horror as one more elephant tried to squeeze on.

Centipede parking lots

Mobile hobbyists

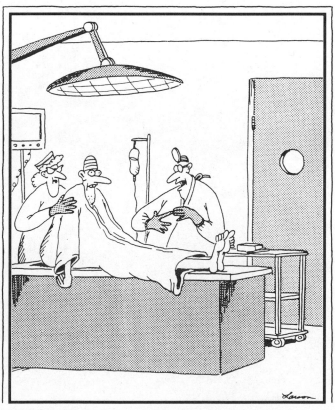

"OK, Mr. Dittmars, remember, that brain is only a temporary, so don't think too hard with it."

"What? You've met someone else? What are you saying? ... Oh, my God! It's not what's-his-name, is it?"

"It's Vince, all right. It's his nose, his mouth, his fur ... but his eyes—
there's something not quite right about his eyes."

And by coincidence, Carl had just reached the "m's."

Hummingbirds on vacation

Cow poetry

"This is no use, Wanda. It's like they say—we just don't have lips."

Our protagonist is about to check on the progress of her remodelers in this scene from "Leona Helmsley Meets the Three Stooges."

"Hey! I'm *trying* to pass the potatoes! ... Remember, my forearms are just as useless as yours!"

"Got him, Byron! It's something in the *Vespula* genus, all right—
and oooooweeeee does he look mad!"

"Man, Ben, I'm gettin' tired of this. ... How many days now we've been eatin' this trail dust?"

"Rex! Don't take it! Everyone knows their mouths are dirtier than our own!"

Suddenly, a heated exchange took place between the king and the moat contractor.

"Barbara, you just have to come over and see all my eggs. The address is: Doris Griswold, 5 feet 4 inches, 160 pounds, brown eyes—I'm in her hair."

"Well, Mr. Rosenburg, your lab results look pretty good—although I might suggest your testosterone level is a tad high."

"Excuse me ... I know the game's almost over, but just for the record, I don't think my buzzer was working properly."

Gus saw them when he crested the hill: snakes. Three of them, basking on the road. Probably diamondbacks.

"Let go, Morty! Let go, Morty! You're pulling me in! ...
Let go, Morty! You're pulling me in!"

"Man, this is havin' no effect. ... But if the boss wants this
varmint dragged through the desert, I ain't gonna argue."

Professor Feldman, traveling back in time, gradually
succumbs to the early stages of nonculture shock.

"Hey! What have I told you kids about screwing around in
front of that window?"

Michelangelo's father

Sucker fish at home

"Wait a minute, friends ... Frank Stevens in marketing—you all know Frank—has just handed me a note ..."

"Yeah, yeah, buddy, I've heard it all before: You've just metamorphosed and you've got 24 hours to find a mate and breed before you die. ... Well, get lost!"

"Well, the Sullivans are out on their tire again."

Broca's brain, appendix, and baseball glove

The class was quietly doing its lesson when Russell, suffering from problems at home, prepared to employ an attention-getting device.

"This *must* be it, Jenkins—the legendary Ugliest Place on Earth."

Bombardier beetles at home

"Step back, Loretta! ... It's a red-hot poker!"

As the small band of hunter-gatherers sat around cleaning their weapons, one made the mistake of looking at his club straight on.

"We understand your concern, ma'am—but this just isn't enough for us to go on. Now, you find the *other* half of your husband, and then we've got a case."

"Farmer Bob. ... Your barn door's open."

The Ty-D-bol family at home

The fate of Don King's great-great-grandfather

Inexplicably, Bob's porcupine goes flat.

"Hold it! There's a car across the street—you sure you weren't followed, Mary?"

Suddenly, the door was kicked open, and with nostrils flaring and manes flying, wild horses dragged Sam away.

"Zorak, you idiot! You've mixed incompatible species in the earth terrarium!"

February 22, 1952: Veterinarians attempt the first skunk de-scenting operation.

"Frances, I've got a feeling we're not on Toto anymore."

"All right! Hand me the tongs, Frank. ... We got us a big den of rattlers here."

"Oh my God, Bernie! You're wearing my nylon?"

Nonunion wagon masters

Runaway trains

Innocent and carefree, Stuart's left hand didn't know what the right was doing.

Scene from the film *Giraffes IV:* This time, they're not just looking for acacia leaves.

Suburban headhunters

Construction birds at lunch

"Oh, professor. ... Did I tell you I had another out-of-head experience last night?"

Nature films that Disney test-marketed but never released.

Frog pioneers

"Well, it's cold again."

"Oh, the whole flower bed is still in shock. He was such a quiet butterfly—kept to himself mostly."

On a clear day, Eugene rose and looked around him and, regrettably, saw who he was.

Punk accountants

Lizard thugs

The heart of the jungle now well beyond them, the three intrepid explorers entered the spleen.

"Good heavens, Bernie! We've got company! ... And you're never going to catch that stupid squirrel anyway!"

Aladdin's lamp, end table, and sofa

Giraffe beach parties

In the corner, Vance was putting the move on two females—unaware that his fake hood had begun to slip.

Misunderstanding his employees' screams of "Simmons has lost his marbles," Mr. Wagner bursts from his office for the last time.

Freudian slide

Semi-desperadoes

"No, no, no! ... That regular rock! Me need Phillips!"

Wharf cows

"Well, I'm not sure. ... I guess it's been washed."

Hopeful parents

The rarely seen victory dance of the poison-arrow frog

Special Agent Gumby falls into the frustrated hands of the enemy.

"OK, Frank, that's enough. I'm sure the Jeffersons are quite amazed at your car headlight device."

Wiener dog distribution centers

147

"*Sure* it's true! ... Cross my heart and hope to die, stick a sharp chunk of obsidian in my eye."

"Aha! The murderer's footprints! 'Course, we all leave tracks like this."

"You need to see medicine man—me just handyman."

"Zak! Don't eat parsley! Just for looks!"

Moses as a kid

Llamas at home

Insect game shows

The untold ending of D.B. Cooper

Just when you thought it was safe to go back into the topsoil.

The famous "Mr. Ed vs. Francis the Talking Mule" debates

"Hey! What's that clown think he's doing?"

Scene from *Bring 'Em Back Preserved*

The four basic personality types

"Who are we kidding, Luke? We know this is going to be just another standoff."

"Well, look who's excited to see you back from being declawed."

"You want me to stop the car, Larry, or do you want to take your brother off the rack this instant?"

The world was going down the tubes. They needed a scapegoat. They found Wayne.

Her answer off by miles, Sheila's "cow sense" was always a target of ridicule.

"Carl, maybe you should just leave your flashlight off. We're trying to scare these kids, not crack 'em up."

"So once they started talking, I just remained motionless, taking in every word. Of course, it was just pure luck I happened to be a fly on the wall."

"Well, here we go again! I *always* get the gurney with one bad wheel."

Times and places never to insert your contact lens.

Danook shows off his Swiss Army Rock.

"Our people are positioned on every street corner, commander. ... Shall we commence with our plan to gradually eliminate these creatures?"

"All this time you've been able to go home whenever you desired—just click your heels together and repeat after me ..."

Bowlers' Hell

"Letter from Lonso. ... And he sounds pretty lonely."

"Well, what d'ya know! ... *I'm* a follower, too!"

"Uh-oh, Bob, the dog's on fire. ... I think it's your turn to put him out."

"Throw him in the swamp? You idiot! That's the *first* place they'll look."

"Oh, for heaven's sake, Miss Carlisle! ... They're only cartoon animals!"

"I tell you I've *had* it! ... I'm not climbing into that getup one more time until you tell me why I'm always the *back* end!"

Sheep health classes

On what was to be his last day on the job, Gus is caught asleep at the switch.

"We must be careful, Cisco! ... Thees could be the eenfamous Queek Sand Beds of Chihuahua."

Scenes from classic nature films

Edgar Allan Poe in a moment of writer's block

Fruitcakes of the World

"Say, Anthony, this looks like a pleasant little place."

"And this report just in. ... Apparently, the grass *is*
greener on the other side."

The tragic proliferation of noseguns

Primitive think tanks

Slowly he would cruise the neighborhood, waiting for that occasional careless child who confused him with another vendor.

"Egad! It's Professor DeArmond—the epitome of evil amongst butterfly collectors!"

Kid shows that bombed

The big-lipped dogs of the equatorial rain forest

Nerds of the Old West

"On three, Vince. Ready?"

Buzzard beakniks

Fly travelogues

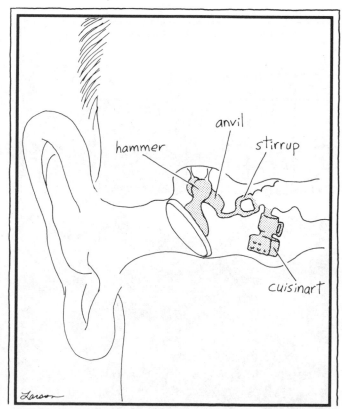

Professor Harold Rosenbloom's diagram of the middle ear, proposing his newly discovered fourth bone.

"Well, there he goes again. ... 'Course, I guess I did the same thing at his age—checking every day to see if I was becoming a silverback."

Forbidden Fruit

Far away, on a hillside, a very specialized breed of dog heard the cry of distress.

The bozone layer: shielding the rest of the solar system from the Earth's harmful effects.

"My God! It *is* Professor Dickle! ... Weinberg, see if you can make out what the devil he was working on, and the rest of you get back to your stations."

Suddenly, two bystanders stuck their heads inside the frame and ruined one of the funniest cartoons ever.